Step-By-Step Tips On

Getting You Kid Into Showbiz

KURTAINS

Without Being Ripped Off

Tia Gold

KURTAINS Copyright © 1998 by Tia Gold All rights reserved. This book or any portion thereof may not be reproduced or used in any manner whatsoever without the express written permission of the publisher except for the use of brief quotations in a book review. Printed in the United States of America Paperback, ISBN 0-9669964-3-2, E-Book Edition, ISBN 0-96669964-1-8, 50 This 50 That Publishing Group 5850 W. 3rd Street Los Angeles, CA 90036 50This50ThatPublishing.com

Acknowledgement

To my mother Debra, my greatest inspiration. Thanks for being a disciplinarian first, honest, strict and for always making me, believe in me. Rest In Heaven, Ma!!

To my son Donovan, thanks for the fun and experience we shared building your career. My son Andrew, thanks for always being there and NEVER leaving my side. To my God-son, Roche Rogers and the play son's I raised hell over, thanks and I love you all!

Norvell, thanks for supporting all of my ideas, even the bad ones. I love you!

To all of the industry executives who cast my children and clients, thanks!

Introduction

Hi, my name is Tia! I'm the mother and onetime manager (momager) of two successful, former industry kids. Both have booked national, and worldwide campaigns in television commercials and as print models, for well-known designers.

My oldest son became the first "Gap" kid, to get cast in a worldwide campaign. He gained notoriety and quickly began earning up to $600 an hour. Soon after, my youngest son booked a national campaign for Nike. Both of their careers flourished. They built themselves a very substantial trust and college fund, thus earning mommy a nice 15% manager's commission. I averaged $90.00 an hour, not bad for mommy duties.

Once I mastered the technique I've written about, I successfully managed a handful of other child clients. The majority became well known and high paid television stars. Today, casting in the entertainment industry is more diverse than ever. The demand is so great for various ethnicities, that now is the time to take advantage of getting your kid on TV.

I'm certain you'll find my technique cost effective, easy to follow, direct, and fun. Good luck on your road to stardom and I look forward to receiving an autographed picture of your child as a result of the KURTAINS, technique!

KURTAINS

To know the industry's right for your child is the first step to getting them into showbiz. There's no one more successful at their craft, than a child whose choice and eagerness it is to do television. Television and print, can both be rewardingly fun and lucrative. On the flipside, it can also be long hard work. A producer will applaud, a kid who's a natural. A child's attitude, who lack's direction, will reveal whether they have been encouraged by an overzealous stage parent or talent manager.

At the age of three, my son was pursued in a department store by a talent scout. While going from one department to the next, I noticed we were being followed. As the woman and I made eye contact, she approached us. The petite blonde was very soft spoken, friendly and upbeat. She wasn't what I pictured a Hollywood talent scout to look like. Conservatively dressed, hair pulled back without any make-up on, she looked more like a school teacher.

No matter how friendly, exercise patience, before becoming too comfortable with a talent agent you are unfamiliar with. Although the majority of agents are reputable, be cautious of those who may not be. There are tons of industry impersonators, who will take advantage of your willingness to make your child a star.

    Being the playful, curious, little boy that my son was, he wandered over to a female mannequin, sitting atop of a table. We paused, and silently watched, as he placed his tiny head under her dress. Unbeknownst to Don, that he was being closely watched by a stranger, he reappeared from under the dress, yelling, "Sexy mama Chiquita"! We all laughed. Thinking it was hilarious, the scout quoted him as being, "Really cute and outgoing". I blushed with embarrassment, trying to explain, he didn't usually do things like that. Donovan wasn't the shy type, and he was full of personality

    As she introduced herself, I was handed her business card. Not leaving any details out, we held a short conversation. I learned who she was, represented, and when to take my son in for an interview. Until this encounter, I personally, had never imagined him being on TV. On our ride home, all I could do was picture him on TV. I could now see him becoming, rich and famous. I saw glitz, glam, red carpet and awards. Not once did I consider whether or not he'd be interested in doing any of it.

    A couple of days had passed, excited, I pulled out the business card that was going to get us to the top. I dialed the number, and asked to speak with the agent. Our appointment, day and time were confirmed. We hung up, I yelled and did what I refer to as a, "Joy dance"! The anticipation of our new found life had almost become unbearable. I spent from that day, forward, trying to figure out what he would wear, how he would get his hair cut, everything, including on down to what he'd say.

Lights, camera, action, it's his time to take center stage. Our appointment day had arrived. My son was perfectly dressed and rehearsed for all that may have been thrown his way. I told Don, to follow mommy's lead and not to worry, we had this. With 30 minutes to spare, we arrived at a well known and very reputable Beverly Hills talent agency. As we stood in the hall, I once again reminded him to just follow my lead, and he agreed.

While sitting in the waiting area, someone came out with a clipboard and asked if I were Donovan's mother, I replied, "Yes, I am". As I was being handed that same clipboard, the woman said, "Great, would you mind filling this out as I take him in for his appointment". "Sure", I said. I sat anxiously and asked if I could fill it out during the interview. She calmly explained, I should do exactly that, but in the waiting area. I was floored, frantic and I panicked. She told me that parents weren't allowed in the room with their child and an agent during meet and greet interviews.

What were we to do? He was in there alone, and was only three years old! And I, being made to wait outside! We practiced everything together. How was he suppose to follow my lead, without seeing it? Alone, he didn't know what to say, not the right thing anyway. There it was, our newfound life, gone!

Parents, brace yourselves for interviews. Having your child go at it alone, is routine for any meet and greet with an agent. This practice is done to measure a child's level of maturity and discipline. No one wants to work with a child who is totally dependent upon a parent.

Inside tip: An agent will often have a desk full of small toys, and trinkets. These things will usually appeal to the average child's eye. Distractions like these, have been put in place to divert a child's attention away from the agent. Remind your five-year old to NEVER touch any of these things and conduct him or herself like a tiny fifty-year old. Maturity and following instructions are extremely important. A child should sit when asked to be seated, and give an agent the best eye contact possible. They should speak only when spoken to, and answer all questions with full sentences. In other words, teach them to not just give one-word answers, this practice will take them a long way in television.

Twenty-five minutes had gone by when Donovan showed his little face again. I was relieved to know the interrogation of my son had ended. The agent called me into her office to discuss the outcome of their interview. She loved him, yes! He did and said all of the right things. Not once did my three-year old touch a single item on her desk. Oh boy, mommy was proud and we're back in the show-biz arena.

TV was all I could think of, up until the point, my son revealed how mature he really was. Closing the interview, she asked Don if he wanted to be on TV and be famous. With a raspy, manlike voice, he politely answered, "No thanks lady, not right now". That's when she informed me, there was nothing more she offers. She advised me to keep her card for the future, in case he changed his mind.

The ride home was numbing. Without ever giving any thought or consideration as to what the desires of my son were, my emotions got caught up in what I hoped could be. The whole way, he talked about the toys on the desk. He told me how much he liked them but didn't touch any of them because I taught him to keep his hands to himself. I just looked over and smiled.

A whole year later, Don now decides he wants to be on television. Commercials, to be exact. Luckily, I held on to the business card from the woman who scouted him. I gave the agency a call and asked for Lucy. The person, on the other end, told me, she was no longer with them and hadn't left a forwarding contact. I was left facing the unexpected dilemma of my son now wanting to be on TV, and me not having a clue as to how I should proceed. I recalled two very key pieces of information obtained during our meeting with Lucy. One, an agent is mandatory, and the other pertained to headshots.

    Lucy informed me that any child not yet represented by an agent, should never have costly, professional headshots taken. Once a child has an agent, you will be referred to a reputable photographer. Most likely, one who will capture that look an agent plans to pitch for a child. Every child's look will rapidly change, between infancy (2 weeks old) and their early tooth shedding stages (up to six years). Instant or disposable pictures were acceptable calling cards, and to audition, your child would need to immediately obtain an agent.

    My next step consisted of sitting Donovan down and discussing our quest. I asked if he was absolutely sure this was something he wanted to do? Was this his own choice and not because anyone else wanted it? He said, "Yes". I explained, it would take patience, a lot of work and time, on my behalf. He agreed to do his best at auditioning, we made it team-work, and began immediately.

    I went to our local drugstore, purchased two black & white disposable cameras and started snapping. Today you have the option of using your cell phone. Just snap, re-snap and print. Black and white photos are an industry favorite because they reflect the truest look to actual life. Your photo's should have as much natural lighting as possible. I'd snap Don when he paid the least amount of attention to the camera. When shooting a headshot, it's important to catch your subject, appearing to look straight at you. This should capture their whole face. Do not to shoot at an angle. If you get only half their face, this will cause the shot to look distorted. When both ears appear in the shot, you have most likely captured a proper headshot.

Choose a comfortable location. A park, the beach, school, home or wherever you and your kid feel is the best place to shoot. Wherever you choose, NEVER let the surroundings or background drown out the main focus, your child. You don't want to capture the big tree behind them, the pretty flowers next to their head, or the big dinosaur slide they're standing beside. Make sure your child's face is the only thing seen in the shot.

When photographing a girl, she shouldn't wear distracting hair gadgets. No cute barrettes or obnoxiously large hair bows. Simple bangs and one or two ponytails are acceptable. Black girls should limit ethnic hair-styles (braids, dreads, etc.). This may type cast your child and limit her potential. Boys should always maintain a neat and clean haircut. A pulled back ponytail, which could camouflage a boy's long hair, is acceptable. Children should never be photographed, holding props of any kind, or with their hands being shown. Clothing should be neat, clean, solid colors, and never displaying any designer logo's. Keep it simple. Do not give your headshot a stereotype. The "Gap" casual look, is always a safe idea. Your child should always depict a look of being from Anytown, USA. An all-American, classic look.

You may have to snap a ton of pictures before capturing the perfect one. It may even take you a few days, locations, and changes of clothes. Be patient, don't rush, it will happen. Don't be hard on yourself or your child, after all, neither of you are professionals. Once you are comfortable, with, at least, one hundred (100) of your best shots, ask a few friends and family their opinions on which they think are best. Once you have narrowed it down to your best three, choose the single best shot. This headshot will be the calling card to securing your child an agent. Remember, submitting unprofessional photos are acceptable, for children who are under the age of six, and or not yet represented by an agent.

Now that you've got your "Money shot", print it on 8x10 photo paper. Be sure to make the appropriate number of copies. Whatever number of agencies you plan to contact, via U.S. mail, is the number of copies you will need. On the photo's backside, in very legible writing, print your child's statistics. Their age, date of birth, height, weight, clothing and shoe size. Your contact information should also be included. Separate from the headshot, includes a short memo. It should state your purpose for contacting the agency. Let them know you are seeking representation for your child, along with the child's talents or experience. Thank them for their time, and how you look forward to hearing from them. Some agencies accept emails. Contact the appropriate agency for their electronic mail submission requirements.

You have the headshot, a neatly typed memo and an 8 1/2 x 11, manila envelope almost ready to go, but who do you mail them to? At the end of the book, I have compiled for you, a list of reputable agencies throughout the U.S. I've also listed a website where you can choose your own. Search for the agency nearest your home town and get started. Inquire about their children's department, current address, and their submission requirements. You can also take advantage of agencies located in other areas. Many families have been known to successfully relocate for their child's career. Feel free to choose as many agencies as you like. You may also want to give google a try. Make sure your choices are reputable. Verify them with the office that governs talent agencies in that city. Address and mail your submissions. Good luck!

This is a sample of what the memo should entail:

Dear Sir,

My name is Jane Doe. I am presently seeking representation for my son/daughter, John Doe. Include your child's talents and or experiences in acting or modeling. Things your child may be exceptional in.

Your contact information. Thank them for their time, and you look forward to hearing from their agency.

Best,

Jane Doe

Some agencies hold open calls. If you call an agency to check email submission requirements, feel free to ask whether they offer open calls. Be ready to take down all pertinent information. If they're offered, they can be extremely beneficial. An open call is a scheduled, opportunity for your child to meet in person with a prospective agent. There will be no need to mail them a headshot. If you get an open call, don't be late, bring a headshot and dress accordingly. The classic "Gap" look is always appropriate unless instructed otherwise. If the agency is interested in possibly working with your child, they will usually convey that during your open call. After an open call, there is NEVER a need to call an agent back, reminding them of your child. This annoys them. A memorable child will not be forgotten. Be patient.

NEVER make a submission to anyone asking you to pay upfront, EVER! You may have to mail up to fifty or more before you even get one reply. You still may not hear anything for a while. Don't let this discourage your efforts to continue. Agents are very busy people. They do not have time to debate over an individual headshot, as to whether or not they have a star. They receive hundreds of submissions weekly. Agents open envelopes and choose the child whose look jumps out at them. Trashing the rest.

Never submit the same headshot to any agency more than once. Doing this will surely get your child's tossed out. Although initially I submitted only five headshots of Donovan, we received four calls back. This I learned was very rare.

During submissions, you may want to consider being, "agency specific". This simply means choosing an agent who represents your child's show-biz interest. If your child wants to be a model, you would then pursue agents who specialize in modeling. Maybe they want commercials only, you would then submit to commercial agents only. If your child is interested in doing it all, your focus should be on agencies who handle clients across the board. Across the board entails everything, motion pictures (big screen), commercials, print (magazines, newspaper, etc.), and runway.

During the time that my boy's we in the business, both were always represented across the board. That kept things simple. Not only that, California has pretty strict rules about having multiple agents. Take New York, for example, you are allowed to have as many agents as necessary. There you have theater and a host of industry branches not offered in California.

Your submissions have been mailed out, and time has passed. Your hard work and dedication thus far could be about to pay off. Your phone rings. It's an agent who received your child's submission. The conversation will be short and sweet. Not a lot of room for questions. Listen very attentively and have what you need at your disposal to take down everything the agent will instruct you to do next. Don't be nervous, never let them see you sweat. These people are usually very nice, especially when it's your child they're interested in.

    I can recall how cool and collected I was when I got a call from one of the former, most prestigious, well-known agencies in the world, Wilhelmina. I took down every bit of information and didn't bother to ask one single question. Like really, what do you ask, Wilhelmina? There was no need, the assistant was extremely thorough in what she needed to relay. Once the call ended, the "Joy dance" was in full swing! WILHELMINA wanted to meet and greet with my son!!! It felt like a prank, it was so surreal.

    This is the call you've been waiting on, treat it as such. Leave no leaf unturned. Have a few questions prepared to ask the agent? They won't mind, ONLY a few. Their main purpose for calling will be to schedule an appointment time, convenient for you all to meet, usually at their office.

    This takes me back to one day, my cousin calling me up, to ask if I would ride with her, and her daughter to a casting call. Quite naturally, I said, "Of course I'll tag along". As we drove to this "Casting", I grilled her with questions. I asked everything from who the company was, to how she learned about the casting. She gave me all of the answers to solidify it being a scam.

As sure as we arrived, all I could see were a sea of people. There were at least 500 kids and their parents. All standing in a long line around a building, waiting to get inside of what looked like a production stage. As we waited, I explained from the looks of things, this wasn't the proper way for her child to get an agent, on commercials or to be a model. Three hours past, when she was asked to fill out a questionnaire prior to the "Screening". What once was a casting call had suddenly become a screening. Whatever you or whoever chooses to call it, it was all wrong.

I spoke with a few other parents who were also standing in line. Some were invited by who they thought were scouts, in a mall or other public, kid friendly place. Others said the radio, TV and some newspapers. I explained to my cousin, that this was all a pitch to get her excited about getting her kid on TV, and then hitting her with either several hundred or thousands of dollars in bogus cost.

Her name was called. We all were permitted entry into the screening. Of course, they had a complete production crew, along with camera people. They gave her exactly what they wanted her to have. A real life experience of being on a sound-stage and seeing her kid on their television screens. The biggest scam I had ever seen involving children. Her daughter made the "Cut" as one "Scout" put it.

Off we went into an office to talk "Business", which really translated into "Cost". Unbelievable, I was outraged!!!

During the "Screening", she was offered all the time she needed to give it some thought. I'm sure, like maybe enough time to think of taking out a second mortgage on her condo, to foot the bill. NO reputable agent would ever pursue talent in such a bogus manner. Paying money will NOT get your child on TV.

So, if you're ever invited by anyone, to a "Screening", to see if your child "Has it", then it's probably a rip-off. Reputable agents, meet in tiny offices without any light, camera, action production equipment. Your child will NEVER, meet and greet an agent in a production type setting, filled with a crew. Productions for talent or fashion shows are not usually put on by reputable agents in search of clients.

I have been on numerous meet and greets with both of my children. Everyone was held in a professional, administrative setting. There were never any cattle call situations. In other words, a reputable meet and greet will never run the Sunday Times Newspaper. Any interested, legitimate agency will contact you personally after receiving your submission.

A recognized agent will NEVER ask for you to pay them upfront, EVER. Agents are only entitled to their contracted commission. Their average rate is usually set at 10% after your child has completed a job negotiated by the agent. An established agency, will do no social media, radio, television, newspaper, mall kiosk or other advertising. They will not offer your child training or workshops, however, agents are willing to refer trusted coaches. Photography services are never handled by, or paid through agents. Neither will an agent split fees with your child's manager.

This appointment may be the most crucial step in your child's career, make it perfect. Both you and your child should rest up the night before, so you will be at your best. Prepare far enough in advance to not be rushed. Be sure you have the correct address, driving directions, and appointment time.

You've arrived at the meeting, your child is the next step closer to securing an agent. Remind your child about not touching trinkets on the desk, taking a seat when offered and speaking when spoken to. Reiterate to your child how important it is to make eye contact with the agent, while speaking. Teach your child to use complete sentences when answering a question (if age appropriate). For example; if asked their favorite color, their response should go something like: "My favorite color is Blue, because it's pretty like the sky". This really shows a child's personality, discipline and ability to follow direction. By only answering with, "Blue" is not leading enough.

Your child's name is being called for the meeting. Relax everything will be fine. The same way my boy's, and every other potential child star went at it, so will yours, alone! Agents are "teacher" friendly professionals, experienced in their field. You will need to fill out a sheet of personal information, regarding you and your child. It's very general but necessary, in case your child is represented by the agency.

Once your child has completed the first half of the interview, someone will summons you into the agents office. All of you are sitting at the trinket-fill desk, the agent may or may not tell you that they are interested in representing your child. Your heart is likely to race uncontrollably. Regardless to what the outcome may be, remain proud of your child.

Fortunately, for us, during the very first meeting Donovan had at Wilhelmina's, they offered to sign him. Of course, we accepted their offer and signed on the spot. No probationary period. The same exact situation occurred with Andrew, at the FORD agency. No sooner than he walked in, they wanted him. Both were contracted, across the board.

During your segment of the meeting, you'll discuss things such as contracts, work permits, work-shops, headshots, auditioning, you and your child's availability, building a resume/portfolio, booking jobs, call backs and SAG. If selected, you may be given a timesheet booklet. This will invoice contractors for the modeling job performed by your child, to ensure they are paid.

Contracts are important factors, which need careful review and consideration. During this initial meeting, it's not likely you will have a contract offered, but possible. Any agent will routinely leave open a ninety-day window before contracting with a new, unsolicited client. I find this probationary period to be good for both parties. It affords everyone the opportunity to see how well they work together, or not.

An entertainment work permit is mandatory for a child to work in this industry. This piece of paper will signify that your school-age child has been granted permission, by the state to be excused from school for the sole purpose of working. Your child may be excused from their school, however, tutoring will be provided on set. Your child's permit must be signed by a school official, indicating he or she has satisfactory grades. At all times, it is very important for your child to maintain a valid permit. For each day that a child is onset working, they must have it their possession. They will not be permitted to report work without it. Proof of a Coogan Account must be attached to the work permit application, or the permit will only be valid for ten days!

When your child makes a ton of money, where will it all go? By law, the only place a minor's money can be placed is in a UTMA, Uniformed Trust Minor Account, also known as a Coogan Account. You can apply for this type of account at your local bank. Check with them to see what their requirements are.

I highly recommend you taking on the task of being your child's manager. As their manager, you will be allowed to receive up to 20% of their earnings. This is sensible, because, not only are you the one who's doing all of the foot-work but footing the cost as well. You can recoup these expenses through managing your child. You do not need any special schooling, certificate or permission if you should choose to manage your child. Twenty percent commission can result in a substantial amount of income. It's surely enough to help with living expenses that can support your child.

Our fifteen percent commission was a win-win for us. It became a way, to teach my boys, the meaning of earning their keep. Parent's must absolutely make sure all of a minor's earning's are deposited into the child's Coogan trust. This leaves no spending, from their earned income. Well, to a kid this might not sound like fun. It'll seem like they're working for nothing. Whenever I received my commission, I would allow the boys to spend from it. This was their interpretation that they worked for it, and should be able to spend or save it. I never explained they were spending mommy's earned income. It worked out extremely well, for all of us.

As a matter of fact, using this concept encouraged my youngest son, Andrew to get into the business. We had gone shopping, and Don purchased himself a quad motorcycle. Andrew decided he also wanted to pick some things up, for himself. I told him, he couldn't buy himself anything, because he had no money. I said, "Donovan works long hours, and he get's paid for doing it." "The money he's spending, he earned, so, therefore, until you earn your income you can't buy thing's of your choosing". He replied, "Mom the next time Don's agent calls, tell her I want to be a model". True story. This is how we discovered he wanted to also be in the industry.

Beginners, ages five and up, should consider workshop training. In fact, I highly recommend it. Children are taught the fundamentals of their craft, along with auditioning technique. Knowing specific commands, will help boost a child's level of confidence while auditioning. The cost of workshops will range from $150 - $200 for a six to eight-week session, meeting one day per week. Usually, on the weekend. A workshop is not mandatory, but helpful.

Throughout their career's, my son's took advantage of commercial workshops. Workshops are just small coaching sessions held for short length's of time. It's not like a college course, where upon completion you'll receive a degree. If they're lucky, they may get a certificate of completion. A cute wall hanger. I found workshops to be beneficial in more ways than one. Sometimes workshop's are coached by casting people. In some cases, casting will be done directly from a workshop. Priority is often given to those whose talents are known by a casting person. (Hint)

Again, professional headshots should NEVER be taken prior to your child securing a reputable agent. Beware of people posing to be legitimate, who take advantage of unsuspecting parents and children. There are many illegitimate companies out there who will attempt to persuade you to purchase high priced photos and other services when they're not needed. After your child gets pass the probationary period with an agent, you will be given referrals to photographer's, usually known by the agent.

Over a period of time, agents establish rapports with many trusted photographers. These photogs will possess the ability to bring out the exact look an agent is intending to cast for their new client. DO NOT have professional headshots taken, then attempt to shop for an agent. The pictures you go out and spend hundreds or even thousands of dollars on, may not be suitable for your child's agent. Your pictures will be trashed, and new ones needed.

Auditions are secured by an agent, through the process known as a breakdown. This is information electronically sent from casting producers to the agent. Information received, will break down a specific type currently being cast for a movie, commercial or print job. An agent will select a client(s) that best fits the character's description. If your child is a good match, their headshot, along with a couple of other clients, will be submitted by their agent requesting audition slots. Whenever a headshot books a slot, a casting assistant will relay this to the agent. An assistant to the agent will give you a call confirming your audition time, place and any other pertinent information needed. You may receive an audition call within hours or days of the call time, availability is key.

Your audition is confirmed, now it's time to prepare. There may or may not be any sides (short section of a script said during an audition) to rehearse. If there are, they may be forwarded prior to the audition, if so, rehearse, rehearse, rehearse! If not, they may be given to you at the audition, just minutes ahead of your call time. Just in case, arrive early enough to go over them.

You've arrived at your audition. The waiting room is small and full of parents with kids running all around. Look for the sign in sheet, sign it. If there are sides, locate them, if not, wait patiently for your child's name to be called. After your child is called, make sure, their headshot is carried along to see the casting agent. Parents are not permitted in the audition, which could take up to fifteen minutes, not much longer.

Once your child enters the casting room, there will be a casting person and possibly a hand full of strangers. Most likely, the others will be a producer and people who are working on the project, along with a camera person if the auditions are being filmed. Your child may meet them briefly, someone will ask for a headshot and resume if one is available. At some auditions, someone may take your child's picture with a digital camera. This is common, so the casting director can easily review all the kids who auditioned that day.

While inside, your child may be told where to stand, which is usually marked on the floor. They will be asked to slate, which simply means to say his or her name, age, and the agency that represents them. The casting person will say when to start, by saying, "Action!" or will say, "Go."

When auditioning for a role on TV, a child who is capable, may read from cue cards. Cue cards are like giant flash cards with words printed on them, in big letters. Your child may also read from sides. Whatever the source is of their reading, they should feel free to do it directly from the script in their hand. Casting people don't mind this, they may even read with you. They're not as concerned with your memory, as they are with, whether or not you fit the part.

Cuteness and beauty may have initially played a part in your child's introduction to show-biz. Personality, along with their ability to follow direction, will help keep them there. In this industry, time is money. No production, large or small is willing to waste either, on a shy or spoiled child. A child who is capable of taking direction on set, wrapping within the allotted timeframe, while their parent(s) are behind the scene, will be called back to work again and again. The industry is pretty tightknit, and word will travel fast, so be sure your potential star is weened off mommy and daddy and can work independently for long hours.

    Upon exiting, your child should thank everyone. If there's a script, hand it back. Parents, before leaving the building, be sure to sign your child out. These auditioning customs are what workshops will teach your child.

    Hundreds of kids with a similar look, has auditioned for the same part, now what? They are all eligible candidates for a callback. Your child may or may not get a callback, if not, don't sweat it. It's important to let a child know how serious an audition is. Never build a child up to feel as if they have to book the job. Children can easily become affected by rejection, just remind them how good they did anyway.

    A callback is more important than the initial audition. This means the director liked your child, so he or she will audition again. I suggest, your child does everything the same way they did at the audition. They should even wear the same exact clothes and hair style. "Break a leg", and hope for a call from the agent. If not, there will be several more callback's ahead.

Congratulations, your child booked the commercial! Great job, in more ways than one. Commercials earn a very good residual income. At least sixty percent of all television income is earned from commercials. Your child has now gotten into show-biz, keep up the good work!

There will never be a magical way of getting your kid into show-biz. Kurtains will provide the most direct technique to getting any child on TV and on their way to earning a great income. I followed each and every one of the steps written in my book, and my son's become a great success.

I'd love to see and hear of your child succeeding at their dream. I am enclosing my personal phone number. You may contact me at (323) 592-0599, Monday-Friday between 11:00 AM and 4:00 PM Pacific Time. I am also available to give advice, answer question's and help in the pursuit of your child's dream, free of charge!

In fact, I'm so eager to see your child succeed, I'm willing to accept your, "Money shot," via email. I'll give it a look-over, a thumb's up or down, with my opinion answered via email. This too is free of charge!

Recognized Agencies:

<u>Atlanta</u>

The Jana Van Dyke Agency 4461 Bretton Ct. #500 Acworth, GA 30101 (770) 529-0655

J Pervis Talent Agency   949 Image Ave Ste. C   Atlanta, GA 30318 (404) 688-9700

People Source   645 Lambert Dr.   Atlanta, GA 30324
(404) 874-6448

Florida

The Hurt Agency 400 N. New York Ave. #207 Winter Park, FL 32789 (407) 740-5700

The Diamond Model and Talent Agency   160 International Parkway #150   Heathrow, FL 32746 (407) 830-4040

Clark Talent   4700 Millenia Bl. #175   Orlando, FL 32839
(407) 233-4481

DMV Area

One Source   7777 Leesburg Pike #3036   Falls Church, VA 22043   (703) 630-3118

iMage International   4959 Hamilton Bl. Allentown, PA 18106   (610) 391-9133

The Bowman Agency   P.O. Box 4071   Lancaster, PA 17604
(717) 898-7716

Texas

Collier Talent Agency   1001 S. Cap of Texas Hwy. Austin, TX
(512) 236-0500

The Campbell Agency   3838 Oaklawn Ave. #900   Dallas, TX 75219 (214) 522-8991

First Models and Talent Agency   9320 Lakeside Bl. Bldg.2 #200 The Woodlands, TX   (281) 363-8146

New York

Clear Talent Group   325 W. 38th St. #1203   NY, NY 10108 (212) 840-4100

Carson-Adler Agency, Inc.   250 West 57th St. #2128   NY, NY 10107   (212) 307-1882

Abrams Artist Agency   26 275 7th Ave.   NY, NY 10001 (646) 486-4600

Tennessee

BNA Talent Group   307 N. 16th Unit. F   Nashville, TN 37206 (615) 457-1164

The Cannon Group   1622 16th Ave. South #500   Nashville, TN 37212 (615) 294-0608

Gage Models/Talent 408 N. Cedar Bluff Rd. #100 Knoxville, TN 37923 (865) 588-8815

Chicago

Gray Talent Group, Inc.   727 S. Dearborn St. #312 Chicago, IL 60605 (312) 663-1659

Stewart Talent Agency   58 Huron St.   Chicago, IL 60654 (312) 943-3131

Grossman & Jack Talent, Inc.   33 W. Grand Ave. #402 Chicago, IL 60654 (312) 587-1155

Los Angeles

Coast to Coast Talent Group 3350 Barham Ave. Los Angeles, CA 90068 (323) 845-9200

Abrams Artist Agency   9200 Sunset Bl.   Los Angeles, CA 90069 (310) 859-0625

L.A. Models   7700 Sunset Bl.   Los Angeles, CA 90046 (323) 463-7700

Louisiana

Clear Talent Group, South   2309 N. Hullen   Metarie, La 70001 (504) 834-8290

J Pervis Talent Agency   P.O. Box 3215   Baton Rouge, La 70821
(225) 329-7775

Detroit

The I Group   29540 Southfield Rd. #200   Southfield, MI 48076
(2480 552-8842

One Source Talent   2653 Industrial Row   Troy, MI 48084
(248) 816-7900

Useful Resources:

Talent Agencies
Agency Verification
http://www.agentassociation.com/

Work Permit Info
http://www.dol.gov/general/topic/youthlabor/workpermitsagecert

Screen Actors Guild Membership Info (SAG/AFTRA)
http://youngperformers.sagaftra.org/files/youngperformers/YPH_FNL3.pdfhttp:/

www.ingramcontent.com/pod-product-compliance
Lightning Source LLC
LaVergne TN
LVHW051207080426
835508LV00021B/2850